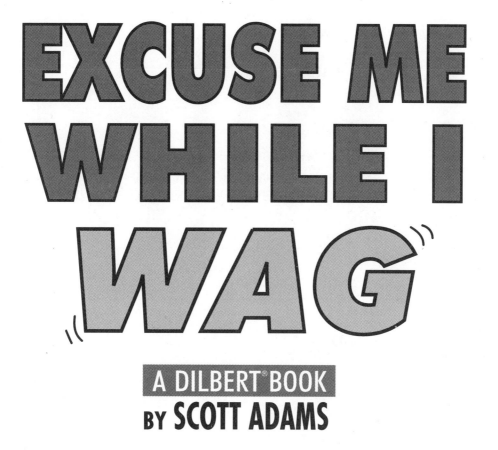

EXCUSE ME WHILE I WAG

A DILBERT® BOOK

BY SCOTT ADAMS

**Andrews McMeel
Publishing**

Kansas City

───── ATTENTION: SCHOOLS AND BUSINESSES ─────

Andrews McMeel books are available at quantity discounts with bulk purchase for educational, business, or sales promotional use. For information, please write to: Special Sales Department, Andrews McMeel Publishing, 4520 Main Street, Kansas City, Missouri 64111.

"This book contains no cilantro."

Introduction

The other day I was at Sears, enjoying the intoxicating fragrance of fresh tools and marveling at the fact that there isn't one best way to rotate a bolt. I think Sears has a whole division of wrench developers who sit around asking questions like, "What if the bolt is in a dark place, around a corner, slightly stripped, guarded by a trained raccoon?" Then someone in the wrench division makes a tool that's part wrench, part flashlight, and part tranquilizer dart gun. All I know is that when they're done, I'll buy three of them—one for the tool bench, one for the car and one in case I lose one.

None of this has anything to do with my point; I just like tools.

Anyway, as I was leaving Sears, I passed a naughty lingerie store and pressed my face to the window hoping to catch a glimpse of some more tools. They didn't have any. But what I saw was very disturbing. It was an employee who, in my opinion, was not the very best fit for the lingerie-selling profession.

Now, before I tell you about this employee, and you judge me to be unkind, let me set the stage with some politically correct self-deprecation: I would like to be a linebacker in the NFL. But because I weigh 155 pounds and have legs like chopsticks I consider myself unsuited for that profession. The list of jobs for which I am not physically suited is very long, including anything that involves lifting heavy objects or having direct sunlight come in contact with my skin.

If I worked at a health club the customers might worry that regular exercise causes people to look like me. If I were a policeman, crooks would take turns beating me up.

This is all a very long way of saying that if you happen to measure your panty size in hectares, maybe you're not the very best choice to work in a lingerie store.

I blame the strong economy. Companies are desperate to fill jobs. They're lowering the bar and tolerating more insolence and disobedience than ever. That's the inspiration behind the title of this book, *Excuse Me While I Wag*. It's an anthem for the new millennium, and it's an attitude you'll notice in Dilbert and his co-workers lately. They're more sassy and sarcastic than in the past.

Speaking of attitude, when Dogbert conquers the planet and becomes supreme ruler, everyone who subscribes to the free Dilbert Newsletter will form the New Ruling Class and make everyone else our domestic servants. The totally free Dilbert newsletter comes out whenever I feel like it, usually four times a year.

To subscribe, send a blank e-mail to dilbert-text-on@list.unitedmedia.com.

To unsubscribe, send a blank e-mail to dilbert-off@list.unitedmedia.com.

If you have problems with the automated subscription method, write to newsletter@unitedmedia.com.

S.Adams

Scott Adams

Scottadams@aol.com
Dilbert.com

11

13

14

26

YOUR WALL IS WARM, MOM.

IS THAT BAD?

THERE'S NO WAY TO BE SURE UNLESS YOU REMOVE THE SHEETROCK AND LOOK.

PLEASE STOP FINDING DEFECTS IN MY HOUSE.

I SMELL PROPANE.

THANKS FOR DROPPING IN. TOO BAD YOU HAVE TO LEAVE SO SOON.

YOUR SIDEWALK IS CRACKING. YOU NEED TO BUILD A DRAINAGE TRENCH, WITH SUMP PUMPS.

WHEN I TOLD HER SHE WAS LIVING IN A POWDER KEG SHE MADE A WEIRD YELPING SOUND.

AS YOU RECOMMENDED, I CANCELED THE SOFTWARE UPGRADE PROJECT.

THAT'S THE EXACT OPPOSITE OF WHAT I RECOMMENDED. YOU ONLY HEAR WHAT YOU WANT TO HEAR.

YES, I DO LOOK THINNER. IT MUST BE BECAUSE OF THE SIT-UP I DID YESTERDAY.

41

WRITE ON A SCRAP OF PAPER THE NAMES OF EMPLOYEES WHO DO GREAT WORK AND PUT THEM IN THE HAT IN MY OFFICE.

AND THEN DO YOU SELECT ONE NAME EACH WEEK TO RECEIVE VALUABLE REWARDS?

NO, THE SCRAPS OF PAPER MAKE MY HAT MORE COMFORTABLE.

EVERY DEPARTMENT WAS ASKED HOW IT COULD REDUCE ITS BUDGET TEN PERCENT.

YOUR PROJECT IS VITAL TO THE FUTURE OF THE COMPANY, SO I CLEVERLY OFFERED TO ELIMINATE IT, KNOWING THEY COULDN'T ACCEPT.

NOW THIS IS THE FUNNY PART...

PHOTOGRAPHY IS MY NEW HOBBY.

CLICK

DO YOU WANT A PICTURE OF ME?

NO, I LIKE TO LOOK AT THEM LATER.

DESIGNING A CALL CENTER

IF THE EMPLOYEES GET THIS VOLUME OF CALLS PER DAY THEY WILL WISH THEY WERE DEAD.

BUT THEY WON'T BE DEAD, JUST TOO BEATEN-DOWN TO LOOK FOR BETTER JOBS.

I DON'T KNOW HOW TO MAKE IT ANY MORE INHUMANE.

WE CAN PUNISH THEM FOR NOT BEING CHEERFUL.

SO, MISTER RATBERT, WHY SHOULD I HIRE YOU TO WORK IN MY CALL CENTER?

I THRIVE ON THE CHALLENGE OF INHUMANE WORKING CONDITIONS.

WATCH ME GO WITHOUT A REST-ROOM BREAK FOR FOUR HOURS!

YOU'RE HIRED.

HERE'S WHERE YOU'LL BE WORKING, RATBERT.

CALL CENTER

THIS MUST BE WHERE PEOPLE LEAVE THEIR SHOES.

IS IT OKAY IF I HANG THINGS ON MY WALL?

THE COMPANY WILL NOT BUY PDA'S FOR EMPLOYEES.

QUESTION: WILL YOU STILL PAY FOR BUSINESS TRIPS OF NO DISCERNIBLE VALUE?

OF COURSE.

A LOT OF PEOPLE ARE TRAVELING TO PALM PILOT CALIFORNIA LATELY.

RRRING

I'VE BEEN WATCHING YOU THROUGH YOUR WEB CAM AND I DON'T THINK YOU'RE WORKING HARD ENOUGH.

WELL, IT WASN'T MUCH OF A FIRE WALL. I'M USING YOUR MAIL SERVER TO SPAM MY MAHJONGG CLUB.

A HACKER BROKE INTO OUR SYSTEM AND FOUND OUT OUR CORPORATE STRATEGY.

DID HE POST IT ON THE INTERNET? I'D LIKE TO READ IT.

I'M ALSO CURIOUS ABOUT MY OBJECTIVES FOR THIS YEAR. DO YOU HAVE THE GUY'S E-MAIL ADDRESS?

76

83

Panel 1: FROM NOW ON, ALL TEAMS WILL BE FORMED ON THE BASIS OF MYERS-BRIGGS PERSONALITY TYPES.

Panel 2: IF YOU DO NOT HAVE A PERSONALITY, ONE WILL BE ASSIGNED TO YOU BY HUMAN RESOURCES.

Panel 3: WE NEED A QUIET DUMB GUY TO PAIR WITH AN EXTROVERTED THINKER.

Panel 4: I HAVE THE RESULTS OF YOUR MYERS-BRIGGS PERSONALITY TEST.

Panel 5: YOU'VE BEEN CLASSIFIED AS A "PHB."

Panel 6: THERE'S A FOURTH LETTER, BUT THAT WAS FOR AN EXPLETIVE.

Panel 7: IN THIS WEEK'S WALLY REPORT, I'LL DISCUSS A SERIOUS THREAT TO MY PRODUCTIVITY.

Panel 8: BY TUESDAY MY BRAIN WAS SO FULL THAT I HAD TO FORGET THINGS TO MAKE ROOM FOR NEW THINGS.

Panel 9: WALLY, I HAVE SOME INFORMATION FOR YOU. GREAT. I'LL JUST FORGET THE FIFTH GRADE.

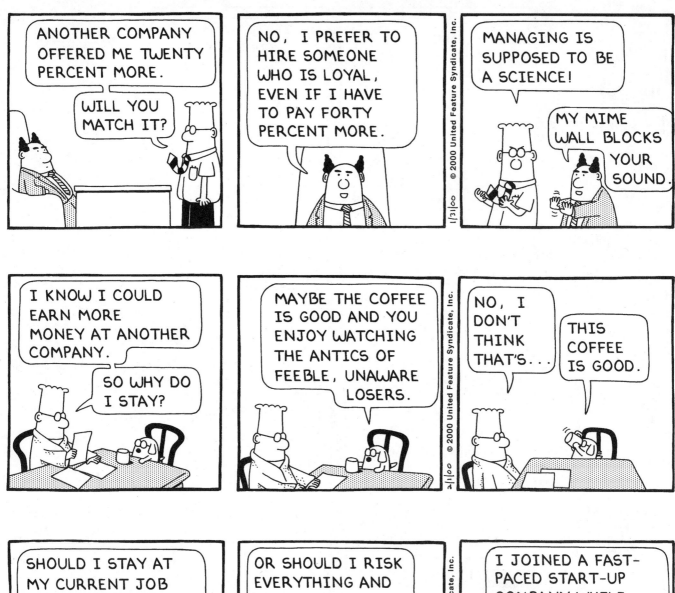

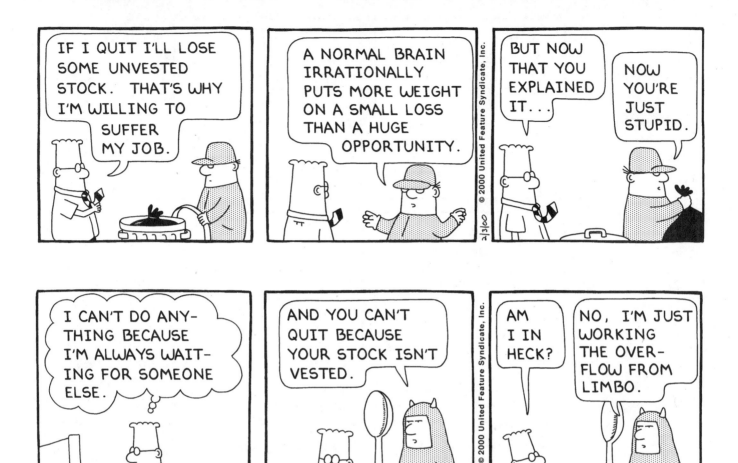

119